Thirsty Bloom

Heather Finton

published 2017 by Northern Undercurrents

ISBN 978-0-9958247-4-4

cover artwork by Lea-Ann Dorval

Compiled in honour of my parents Sue and Ross and their 50th wedding anniversary.

While love dances in different shapes on these pages, it has been a deep privilege to witness it dancing on their faces for decades.

I take refuge
in the whiteboard
in my body

the blank page
where I gently wipe clean
all the lovely thoughts
and painful stories

where the pastel shades
and violent hues
of sensation and emotion
show their colours
and leave no trace

where I trust
that even scintillating awe
and the wonder of star-song
will return in good time
and just now I can wipe their beauty
away

there is freedom
moving through the eraser
and my choice
to keep tending
this empty space.

It is hard
to shrug off a shell,
beetling your way
up a hill, all alone

aware of the press
of your own muscles,
the knots of your own making,
patterns of strong protection

and noticing
how sturdy insects
need a carapace.

What quiet joy
to fall helpless,
to feel the shell
roll to ocean,
water filling
and emptying,
surrendered on the shore;
a home just slightly less tethered,
waves of freedom
altering its shape.

Gaia be laughin'
tellin' all the women
to smile,
whisperin' to menfolk
to be strong
the way of spiderwebs,
fragile 'n' connected.

Gaia be stretchin'
slow roll of hillsides
wavin' her arms like treetops,
lazy 'n' patient in love,
pointin' to freedom.

Gaia be chucklin'
brooks you can drink from,
makin' space for grimy faces,
hands that need washin'
before they are cupped.

Gaia be feelin'
moonlight 'n' sunlight
turnin' 'n' churnin'
warmin' 'n' coolin' both sides
always,
held 'n' holdin'.

Have you heard the news?
Listen to the leaves,
they'll tell you
- they're excited
in their patient, rooted thrumming

they murmur in the night
whispering delight
over sleeping feathers
and all who stalk and scamper
under the moon.

Have you heard the news?
The planet is alive,
our cells
are full of love
for us
and all her kin.

Have you heard about the woman
who moved thousands of miles
from her home
to speak out
for our right to choose who to love?
Did you hear about the one
who travelled over tar sands
to scoop up music
out of the muck?

Did you hear of the woman
whose sorrow ran so deep
that only tears could save her?

4

Have you heard of the women
with grey in their hair
and bounce in their step
who generously bestow
fierce blessings?

Did you hear about the children
carried inside women
who will birth them soon
in a world
that will be different
from now?

Did you hear
about the thousand eyes
and ten thousand lifetimes
that swirl in your DNA
and propel you with infinite
tenderness?

Did you hear the news, rustling?
Will you share news?
What will you make new?

As this movie
gets more intense
I realize the theatre
is changing

these seats!
how plush and sensuous
and perfectly formed
to change with me

and these companions
who hold my hands
in the dark

and I don't know
why they brought in
such a wonderful chef
for the popcorn

...the movie itself
has brighter colour,
even grey looks more lovely
than it used to

and how deeply I can cry
and laugh
and admire the cinematography

and know where I am in it.

Snuffling and large,
these horses stamp hooves
in the corral of my heart,
scaring me
with their intensity
and smelling of animal,
hungry and dangerous.

I have no skill with the whip,
no farrier's touch,
and have been known to stumble,
to drop my small bucket of oats.

Today I must stand
on the safe side of the fence,
watching them pound in frustration,
feeling my fear.

Not enough apples,
this one I hold
in a fragile but open hand
can be extended
with hope of more.

Actually
you can

drop the conversation
of easy or hard

step out
from behind

listen
to which foot
will lead

and then move it

wait
to notice the need
to inhale

let your lips
receive instruction
and then mould air
into sound

your courage
is right here

inviting life.

Let the universe
do its job

the life force swells
underneath you,
around you

nudging you into love
like dolphin and ocean.

Relax
into gravity,
let orbits spin
while you sit still,
know that you are moving
without effort.

There is winking
all around you,
trying to catch your eye

receive these glances
with freedom,
incline your crown
with reverent thanks,
grin back.

It is raining
in my house,
heat from the woodstove
melting unnoticed ice,
a thaw full of dripping
and gurgling.

The whole back body
of the stove
was frozen,
encrusted in thick white
and hidden from view

only the heat
revealed it,
making ice known
by the unexpected sizzle,
water drops on warmed metal.

What looked like a cozy home
had a snowy corner,
not a deception,
just a cold patch unrevealed.

May this melting be a mirror
to see my own back
in plain view
without contortions,
finding fuel for necessary fire,
patience in change.

Was there laughter
between them
when she touched
the hem of his robe?

Did he spin
to find her
no longer cowering,
eyes dancing
with the mischief of her healing?

I'd always heard that story
as if she bravely stole
and he forgave

but woke today
to the joy of it

his delight
in feeling love move

her momentary bliss
in receiving.

Something about sheep
and how I have been
shepherding,
trying to safeguard
and be vigilant,
wary of predators
and dark nights

how I count with every dawn
these precious names,
watching for what needs feeding,
proper shearing,

responsible
for all these rams and ewes and
lambs.

A shock, then,
to see they are not mine,
their dances with wolves
out of my hands,
their journeys and wool
for an owner beyond my ken.

My daily walk continues,
unsupervised, unpaid;
I can choose lute or whistle
for my comfort
as I tend
the fires I light at sunset.
Bleating and nuzzling
sound unchanged;
my ears receiving
and offering
gifts that were never mine.

12

Semaphore

So actually, God,
who does not exist
the way the word
would suggest,
not a singular entity
but a wild multiplicity
crystallized
in fluid oneness,

anyhow this God
(infinitely beyond personality,
wearing this word
like a ballcap
just to satisfy this pen)

is trying to catch your eye,
flashing all this gorgeous
semaphore
that may not yet get your attention

so asked me
to ask you
to notice.

Percussive

Acolyte of mountains
she learned much from their
strength,
the way their height
looms from unseen depth,
play of light and shade
on sloped canvas,
turnings of day
and season.

Today her feet thump
to pound a new staccato,
pushing against what is solid
with springtime agitation,
letting muscle and bone
sing a real song,
make uncomfortable music,
releasing what is here
to make new space.

Authentic,
this indoor pacing,
bare soles on different kinds of floor,
aimless and alert,
an unsoothed meditation,
percussive wandering.

Aspects

Martha and Mary
compete for space.

Martha is incensed
by the way her sister
refuses to engage,

the bickering one-sided
and hanging ignored
like a corner without air

this home too small
for Mary to wander

too messy
for Martha to rest.

Sometimes they have joined forces
smiling at each other's need,
a broom and a poem
filling the house with different kinds
of light

but lately
they are both brooding,
squatting on nests
that feel empty

not sure where to push.

Array

All those telescopes in tune,

filling a field,

expectant listening,

receiving and distilling,

attentive and moving by fractions,

planted and supple

and not just yin,

but also thrust,

the vivid squint skywards

beyond what is known,

the questing thirst

to find new edges

from which to stretch

the field collective,

harnessing the brightest on offer,

pooling vigilance and spark,

patience and push,

mirrors sharing perspectives,

eternal changing views.

For a long time
I thought peace
meant feeling calm and happy

trying to cheer
my serious face.

Now I understand
that sighs
don't need a story,
breath escaping body
as it is,
no reason
for happiness
or sadness
even as both
share space.

Hope

The Greeks said
it's the only bright light
left in the box,
Pandora's treasure
for humans
to carry

while the Buddhists said
it will kill you
in a frenzy
of waiting for tomorrow

and me,
I need both
inhale and exhale,
trust in what could come
as healing,
tending to the open wounds
right here

finding beauty
in their serrated edges,
the colours of pus and blood,
old and fresh and future
intermingled.

Today I saw it happen,
light crawled tenderly
across the walls,
creeping with kindness
over the space where I live.

The sky
had already turned to day,
but these were the knees and
elbows
of dawn fully launched,
making itself known.

A different shade of bright,
warm with glints of laughter,
changing the colour
of everything that did not move
and the shape of my grin.

There was a dome
over the decadent hot pool
in the temple for beauty
where I lounged yesterday

not just pampered
but also paying homage
to divinity

the deep ablutions,
supplications
from open cells
and silent whispers.

Like any sacred space,
profane participation too,
rote customs
and new immersions,
money changing hands
for services rendered.

We choose to engage,
or perhaps we are chosen,
to feel the subtle weavings,
to notice the impossibility
of bricks
circling in sky,
conveying light.

Because Jacob asked

Somehow life decided
to gather bubbles
full of effervescent light

and wrap them tenderly
in resilient skin,
a lithe body
determined

crowned with copper splendour
glinting in his eyes
and amazing grin

these bubbles
like jet fuel,
propulsion into joy.

The way the deer jumped
in front of my car
with enough graceful timing
I only had to watch
without panic
and we both moved on;

the way there is only one bowl
of leftover salad
and I am the only one
who wants it
and it is lovely;

the way two chairs broke
under two large men
on the same day
and neither fell to the floor;

the elegant sufficiency
in which we are suspended
will even be a cushion
if we let it.

Pick me up
by the scruff,
shake me
on this journey

letting me feel
the loose camouflage
of this skin,
the jumbled bones
within

the helpless hanging,
alert and shining eyes

willing to be carried
to safety,
set down
in new alignment.

So much of what felt true
has tumbled,
I would be adrift
but for this warm bite
near my wobbling spine,
surrender to a voyage
with paws resting briefly in air.

Ordination

Long stretches of my ballad
were etched by my longing
to be anointed

to receive a special blessing
for some deep authority

God's thumb on my forehead
or vocation with map

then one day light
poured on me and my sisters,
a circle of singing,
crones and maidens interlinked
raw tender

a holy oil uprising
as benediction
I could not hide from

supplication over
gift welcomed.

Like a salmon
nosing my way upstream
to find the full force
of unobstructed flow

there are ways of being stuck,
bumping against protection

using my obstacles
to rest behind,
wishing I could stay
in a smaller place.

I see it too
in the longing of my friends
who believed that clocks
could be fixed or discarded

who knew that rules
would keep them safe
who trusted that the mind
was rational.

Our disposable society
can learn from the simple cocoon:
not to stitch uselessly
against necessary change,
finding grace
in the fall of organic husks,
new pulsing underneath.

And you, my friend in pain,
let go the self-inflicted needle;
let your wounds show
uncovered,
your wet colour unfurl.

I can't find my glasses
again

and blurred vision
softens
my usual precision

the dawn would look more intricate
if I could better see
where light touches shadows

I know that there is more
going on
than my natural eyes
can perceive

this croaking
is a song
about relaxing in real life

blurred vision
gentle and here.

A stoplight
and all the advertising,
more litter than usual
filling the gutter
after snow's departure,
grey gravel

and I looked up
to see five northward swans,
organic alignment

isn't that the way.

I can't even talk about love
with all its layers,
the word too encrusted
with rusty protections

disarming metaphors
flutter like old leaves
tossed by spring

snowmelt in a gutter,
flowing and grey,
barely refracting light

the way freestyle
means crazy propulsion
into possibility, airborne

an old man
in a big truck
chewing his finger like a child

lovers with no muscle tone,
soft flab of years
sharing a bathtub

the sparkle in your eyes
catching mine.

All these rips and tears,
the scratched faces
of my bruised neighbours,
the slow foggy clouds
that envelop us all...

this is part of the reason
it feels easier
to sleep,

awareness of my wounds
and all these suffering others
too damn much
to carry.

And while this is true
and does not go away,
a shaft of sunlight
also pierces,
quirking my lips
in remembrance
of our collective staggering,
how we none of us carries it all,
how we are also carried.

Two souls enraptured,

glowing like old cans

punctured

so the candlelight

flows new patterns

on the walls

reflected radiance

from a ceaseless flame

light embodied

in ten-fingered touch

and tongues that lick profusely

a deep rough kindness

finding home.

They call it dancing
but lately I want
another word,
a river of sounds
to echo my gratitude.
or bubbles to wrap
these particles of freedom
into something floating
and visible.

I have been so moved
by music's entry
into my bloodstream,
the invitation to muscle
to try so much that is new,
to laugh at constraint
and wiggle again,
to pound and snap
knowing
that practice
does not mean rehearsal.

We don't read many poems
about what the vacuum sucks
or the not-quite-written
marketing plan,
or the ski camp registration
overdue.

Sometimes
the grey green fuzz
like a garden
using vegetables as soil in my fridge
becomes a cold and verdant
doorway
into where I am,
prolific in decay.

Today these are not beginnings,
not endings,
unfinishable business
nurturing my attention.

A lawn sprinkler
like a tractor
moving slowly along the path
of its own source for giving

using the hose
as a guide

propelled by all
it offers,
dispersing

sometimes hesitant
without pressure
or going rogue,
off the trail

it moves so slowly
I am forced to change
the way I watch it

mirror my own watering.

I used to ride the train
the way so many do,
hurtling forward
to a future place
as if all the sights
outside the window
were real.

Then I learned to walk the track,
to wander on the way
more slowly,
pausing to fall on my knees,
press my ear to the ribbon,
gleaning awareness
of what was coming.

Now I feel the tug
of the lateral journey,
stepping off the rails
to the flowers and brambles,
releasing my promise
of forward motion,
sitting on unfamiliar ground
with open eyes
while birds and trains
keep moving.

I am weird
and this hunched heart
with its babbled apologies
is just trying to hide
the fact of my strangeness.

Of course we're all weird
but my own particular oddness
seems like it might be
offensive
or make waves

or scare others
as much as it scares me.

Yet today
I have the open-hearted kindness
to welcome myself deeply

and take my place
with all the weirdos
and laugh
at the sight of us.

Pelvic relaxation
sounds nicer
than a prolapsed uterus

this search for what is nice
and more comfortable

the way the world
is all about perception

we choose
our illusions

and life keeps offering
soft weak hands
for our grasping,
allowing us to let fall.

Sometimes I bump my nose
on a doorframe
that seemed to come out of
nowhere
or trip
on a cord
and feel the smack of ground.

Other times I see the stage
and watch myself bumbling,
noticing my patterns.

Still other times
I feel the canvas sling
of the director's chair,
plotting and marking
more beautiful scenes,
collaborating with an invisible author.

Every day
I try to be the page,
even for a few precious seconds,
the blank sheet
before any story.

The truth of not enough

My petulant self
the one who mostly hides
her stomping foot

a tantrum child
enraged by injustice,
how life is not fair...

my home is larger now
and she can stomp
with room for me to hear her.

Her truths are less dangerous
than the barricades,
her whining less shameful,
my wisdom heart
can honour her passion,
distill her drops of insight
from a toxic brew.

It's true that you will never love me enough,
will never see from inside these eyes,
will never be a harp and harpist
all in one moment.

Let me savour this burning
like a flaming shooter,
a warm forbidden pleasure,
fueling my fire.

And laughing,
rise from my taste of bittersweet
to raise my empty glass in your honour,
curious.

That bird
is out of its range,
much higher
on the rooftop
than its kind would have it.

I watched its progress
from railing to railing,
climbing the balconies
in short steps
as nature intended

am curious
to see what happens next,
what flight
and landing
from such an odd vantage.

A real lotus
will wilt,
turning brown at the tips
of its loveliness,
folding inwards
when the mud
no longer feeds it,
experiencing decay
with just as much gentle passion
as the upwards dance.

In the sinking,
while loveliness changes
into something present with its own
descent,
there is a freedom
in the dying roots,
a tenderness of toes
that feed the soil
through no attempt at nurturing

a joyful acceptance
of the death-dance,
the way the mud requires
more nutrients
for what comes next.

Let my soul grow legs;
for too long
I have wavered inside
like luminescence
bouncing sidesaddle
on an unruly horse,
controlling and rejecting
my own ride.

Deep inside,
an unseated wobble,
confusion about home,
sadness over limitations.

Let my soul descend
through roiling belly
and find the fit
of exquisite thighs and feet
tailored perfectly for me

submit to the wisdom
of the horse I have also been
and ride this waiting saddle,
this new seat.

I have the right
to feel this way

who ever suggested
I didn't?

Where did I learn
that feelings were legislated?
or property of some collective,
a gated community?

I feel more than one thing
right now,
emotional notes
forming this changing music

and they are free
for the tasting

so let me lick.

Jostled by my neighbours
I am invisible

the eye looking at shoreline
cannot see me,
makes no distinction
whether I am submerged
or dry and baking
or how these moments of moisture
change throughout the day
with ebb and flow of tide

and still we keep imagining,
perception of ocean and shore
as if we stride between them

forgetting our smallness,
how we are each one fleck,
one speck,
a particle of shifting earth,
insubstantial and real,
rubbed and rubbing.

Two birds flying
pell-mell through bushes
almost like bats
narrowly missing branches

no flight plan
such intensity of speed

one in front
the other following
precise imitation
of convoluted path

was she in front
and being chased?
leading him onwards?

reflecting from behind his every
move?

So curious to know,
often I forget
my own flapping.

44

Like parallel play,
the deep game
engages my attention

forcing me to speak
in new voices

asking me to stretch inwards
for rescue

to crawl slowly
and go nowhere,
relishing
the crunch of my knees

and somehow
the butterfly effect
lets my dreams
be travelled
in more than one way,

lets my friends
be touched
in moments that look random

hold their hands
inside my belly

or when we bump.

If we were in a ring
wrestling fully immersed
I know I'd lose
broken and bleeding

I really don't trust
that we have shared rules
or recognize a referee
or listen to a bell

there is a kind of greed
that feels insatiable.

For too long
I have laboured in silence
or used words like shards of glass
to try to tame you out of violence
into a ring where the mat is safe,
ropes visible and respected.

This sport like all craft
has much to teach me;
I am not ready
to trust you as my teacher

but have found new trust
that we are both learning.

I used to swim
with a life ring
secure on my middle

awkward but safe
above the salty water

now I swim without it
but still make my way
often
to the rafts and buoys
dotting the bay,
my goals and fixes
in plain view,
the primacy of purpose.

And yes, in storms
I am grateful
for these small protections
and places to cling.

More recently
the waves are calm enough
for floating,
understanding that destination
is meaningless,
water carries,
immersion is possible
in storm
or gentle sea.

There is room
for your beauty
right here beside me

come sit
and let your petals relax,
unfurl your jagged thorns
as mine will not wound you further.

Yesterday I heard a poem
spoken with such passion,
pointing to expansive life,
pouring my joy and longing
through a finely crafted jug

my own urn seemed too small
as gaia splashed out

and I thought my pen
would never move again.

This rubbing and bruising
and silence
marks my dance with the divine,

love in celibate form
even in marriage

passion pooling
in a hidden cavern
for a new kind of swimming

invitations to love without owning,
no acquiring

huntress dropping her bow
to swim alone.

48

This warm spring
makes loneliness seem like a joke;
crowded with the presence
of so many lovers
immersed in living

a fertile celibacy,
fecundity in recognition,

a body buzzing
provoked by the glance of love
in a squirrel's eye,
a child's grubby hand,
a stranger's smile.

If you have rocks in your belly,
sit still
and you will notice
how they ring around water
you can put a toe in

that pool
will expand for your immersion
it is not going anywhere
just like you
it lives here and is part of you.

Sit, let your petals relax,
let it feel like too much
and know that's universal;
know that the floor
will catch you;
there is room for your beauty
right here.

Dreaming,
I was playing a game
with cool graphics
and lots of movement;
adrenalin was flowing
and it was all about tactics,
how to gather more points
and win at war.

And then it shifted,
became a dream about what we
teach
and whether we offer
something different

how we can wake our children
with a game of war
or a palette

how the possibilities
of colour and brush
are endless

and though it felt a little early
to rise from my lazy bed
I could tell
it was time to wake up.

The wag end of a dog,
the flick of a tail
pointing to instinct
and pleasure
expressed by the planet
through years of evolution
in one brief wave

so much of what I do
the same involuntary movement

except the planet can see it
when I do

having evolved these inner eyes
I choose to open

volition more ancient than me
wagging my tail.

www.ingramcontent.com/pod-product-compliance
Lightning Source LLC
Chambersburg PA
CBHW071740020426
42331CB00008B/2108